Midnight Owl

Liz Gent

A catalogue record for this book is available from the National Library of Australia

Text Copyright © 2023 Liz Gent
Illustration Copyright © 2023 Liz Gent
All rights reserved.
ISBN-13: 978-1-922727-99-2

Printed by Linellen Press
265 Boomerang Road
Oldbury, Western Australia
www.linellenpress.com.au

Dedication

I dedicate this little book of poems to my lovely mum and my hubby Patrick. I only wish they were here in person to see the poems in print. I know they would be chuffed, and I thank them both for their support and encouragement over the years.

Contents

Dedication iii

Contents v

A Present for Mum – She's Not Been Well 1

The Sweep's Visit 4

Ode to a Commode 7

The Dag's Tale 8

The Sore Back 11

Beck, the Golden Butterfly 14

John and his Tangled Jib 16

Trouble in the Veggie Patch 18

The Royal Encounter 21

Geoff and the Tale of the Fish 22

I am a Piece of GI Tubing 25

A Blob 26

Mammogram –'Two-Up' for Beginners 28

When I was Nine 31

The Pap Test 34

Wind in the Pillows 36

A Finger in a Bandage 42

Detecting a Problem 44

The Sad Story of the Knicker Elastic 46

A Staffy Loves a Garden 48

My Dentist, my Friend 50

I Couldn't Find a Leprechaun 53

I've Done in Both my Shoulders 56

I'm Turning 70 62

The 3 Wise Poops 64

Movement at the Joint 65

Peter and Me at PRC 68

Me and the 'Butterfly Queen' at PRC 69

My New Glasses –the Eyes Have It 71

Does it Rain in Heaven? 75

About the Author 77

A Present for Mum – She's Not Been Well

It was on the 17th October
I went to the shops for me mum,
I bought something I thought useful,
it earnt me a kick up the bum,
She'd said "I want milk, pills and potatoes
don't bring them covered in dirt,"
I went and did as she told me –
that's how my rear end got hurt!

I got bread, milk and potatoes
from a friendly Indian man,
Then I spotted my downfall –
evaporated milk in a can!
I'll get one of those for my mummy
(I didn't want her to be short)
I staggered back home with my pressie
and shouted, "Guess what I bought?"

Mum's face went all pale and peculiar
when I emptied the trolley at home,
She went sort of red and blue blotches,
then she started to foam,
"You've been done, you daft chump!" she shouted
as I turned to jelly in fear,
I thought she'd storm up the shop
and poke the bloke in his ear.

"He's charged far too much money
– this tin is 79p,
You can buy the same at Tesco
for half the money you see!"
Tomorrow my mum's going to visit
That daft little shop herself,
I bet his evap milk will be splattered
all over him and his shelf.

So when mum tells you to buy her
milk, pills and pot's,
Stay clear of evaporated milk …
it's bound to give her the hots!

The Sweep's Visit

It was a windy day in November –
this story I tell you is true,
The sweep came with his son
to unblock mum's troublesome flue.
Me mum thought the coal was all crappy
(the ashes all went to stone)
She got in a rage and decided
to tackle the sweep on the phone.

He said "I'll be there in a fortnight
at roughly a quarter to 2"
He came with his kid and his brushes –
all black as an elephant's poo!
The son put a brush on the rod's end,
and shoved it with glee up the pipe.
The dad rushed outside in the garden
to see that the soot was all ripe!

A black cloud of soot filled the kitchen,
all four of us covered in mire,
The sweep said "There you are, Mary,
clean pipe makes for a good fire!"
The men cleared the plastic and brushes
and started to move out the door,
Soot was in every small corner and cupboard –
we cleaned until quarter to 4!

So if you have trouble with boilers
and your coal won't give off its heat,
Call out Soden & Soden…
they'll brush out your flue pretty neat!
But a word of warning in closing,
don't upset your sweep at his chore,
He just might take umbridge at comments,
and drop his brush on the floor!

Ode to a Commode

My mum has a faithful companion
that deserves both a song and an ode,
It stays in the corner at night-time –
her partner, a little commode.
This potty on legs is a Godsend,
it never complains or swears,
And if too many visitors roll up,
you can use it as one of your chairs.

It's silent, free-standing and faithful –
don't freeze in the winter, that's true,
She says "it's only for weeing …
I never use it for number two!"
Mum sometimes finds it quite handy
to hang all her cardigans on,
She won't leave clothes there at night,
"my clothes take on a pong!"

There is a small danger at dark time
if you use the pot in the night,
To feel your way when you're sleepy –
the lid could be ever so tight.
But tightness is not the real problem,
it's whether it's been used, that's the fright!

The Dag's Tale

When I first came to Australia,
I was so raw and new,
The story of this rawness
I'll now relate to you.
I've always been a Pommy,
British through and through,
I have now discovered
a bit of me's true blue!

My friends all think I'm silly
 and call me silly bag,
But now I've found it's different,
now I'm just a dag.
I went to Perth to Myers,
Aherns and Strandbags,
Couldn't find a one of them
to tell me what are dags.
What is a dag, I wondered…
could they have one at the zoo?
So, notebook at the ready
I went to see – it's true.

The keeper started laughing
when I asked about a dag,
Does it fly or squawk or flutter –
can you keep it in a bag?
The man was nice and helpful,
took me round to see the sheep,
I said "Oh warm and lovely woolly,
and they are all asleep."

He poked a sheep most gently so it
stood upon its feet,
Then he carefully showed me a dag...
so very very neat.
I took a look and scarpered
at this wondrous find,
A dag's a blob of sheep dung –
stuck to its behind!

The Sore Back

When God invented bodies oh so long ago,
He also made a back bone – there begins my woe.
Muscles are delightful, blood is juicy too,
But damage to your back knocks you out,
that's true!

I'd been so very careful lifting people off the floor,
It was a work of art getting through the door.
I felt a tiny twinge, really just a jar,
when I pulled a patient halfway out the car.

I had a small spasm, not a great to do,
When four vollies and a patient got
stuck inside the loo.
Wes and I were singing to help the patient wee,
I was really moaning as they were sat on me!

I did my dash at Clinic then needed a little rest,
So I dug my daughter's garden,
the back it stood the test.
So then I moved the rubbish
piled in our garden shed,
Now I write this tale from my lovely cosy bed.

The back's had every muscle pulled
and jerked about,
The Dimples of Venus ache
and make me want to shout.
I do a bit of crying and moaning from within,
But Panadeine is great, and so is Naprosyn!

My water bottle's freezing and I'd like a cup of tea,
It takes me thirty minutes
to shower and have a wee.
Knickers are a challenge
when they are on the floor,
So I can reach them easy I hang them on the door.

I've given up on eating, it's not much joy in bed,
My stomach's really empty – waiting to be fed.
I've had some tea and cornflakes,
they're good for you I'm told,
Nothing more exciting
than tea that's freezing cold!

It's time now for my shower,
the challenge of the day,
The floor is clear of towels – nothing in the way.
No bending, lifting, stooping,
the doctor was most clear,
Oh damn! Now I've gone and poured
shampoo in my ear!

My sense of balance left me
and I slipped down to the floor,
At least my clothes are down there,
I couldn't ask for more.
Just an hour later I've achieved this wondrous task,
And back to bed I crawl, its comfort there to bask.

This tale of woe is a warning
to all of you out there,
A back's a friend forever,
so please of it TAKE CARE!

Beck, the Golden Butterfly

Once upon a rhubarb leaf there was a tale to tell,
A story of a miracle that started out in Hell.
A quiet little creature with problems very true,
Her metamorphic journey
I will now share with you.

It was a very rainy day on the rhubarb leaf,
Underneath its shelter a grub had come to grief –
The stalk was wet and slimy,
the grub ran out of luck,
Down amongst the daisies you could hear
"Oh firetruck!"

A frog named George was passing
on his way to shop,
Leaning down picked up the grub
and helped her to the top.
"Oh, thank you," said the little grub
to her newfound friend,
"You're welcome, dear," the froggy called
as he hopped off round the bend.

The little grub was sleepy
as she gazed up at the moon,
With dawn softly breaking –
she'd become a brown cocoon!
Time went by in the garden
and Spring arrived at last,
The sun had brought the flowers,
and melted Winter's blast.

The little cocoon was trembling,
her sides began to split,
The case was bursting open …
she could no longer fit!
"I think I might be dying,"
and gave a mighty sigh,
But no, the little grub
was now a butterfly!

A sight so rare and lovely, shades of gold and blue,
The sunbeams changed her wings
to every type of hue.
"I'm reborn and so happy with joy inside my heart,
I've been given new life, a Fresh Start!"

John and his Tangled Jib

John was a clever surgeon,
a doctor through and through,
He wanted to be a sailor
and sail the ocean blue.
So he and two companions
set out one sunny day,
Sadly for John, disaster
was waiting in the bay.

"Lower the jib and main brace,
bring the boat about"
They looked at him in horror
as he gave a strangled shout,
His arm was squashed by cabin door
and he was all a quake,
"Don't stand there looking silly,
I think I've got a break!"

With gentle hands and ripped up sail
they tied the broken bone,
John, the doctor, really calm
was on his mobile phone.
He'd phoned his wife and told her
not to make his tea,
They'd go straight down to Charlie's
and have his arm pain free.

The moral of this story –
safety is the key,
Watch what you are doing
when you're out at sea.
Don't gaze up at the seagulls,
or hear the dolphins sing,
Or you'll end up just like John,
arm done up in a sling.

Trouble in the Veggie Patch

It was quiet in the garden,
all the bugs were fast asleep,
All except for one,
who was lying in a heap,
Perhaps it was the weather
or maybe just her mood,
This bug became unhappy
and yelled out for some food.

"Give me food, I'm hungry,"
she cried with angry face,
Her friends, the other bugs,
ran about the place.
They brought her lettuce grown nearby –
a stroke of such good luck,
But in response all they got was
"Oh, firetruck!"

A caring bug with glasses said,
"Let me help you, dear."
Her kindness was rewarded
with a thump upon her ear.
The other bugs were angry
and told blue butterfly,
That one of them was hurt
and had been made to cry.

Butterfly thought carefully:
"that bug, she needs to sleep"
Upsetting all the garden
and making someone weep.
He looked inside his handy bag
and gave a little smile,
"One of these will do the trick,
she'll sleep now for a while."

Peace wafted to the garden,
and gentle snores were heard,
The pill had done its magic –
so quiet, nothing stirred.
I'd like to say that all was good
and she was troubled less,
But no, within the hour
she'd taken off her dress!

The bugs were full of caring
and dressed her up again,
Filled her up with lettuce
and took away her pain.
As sun set in the garden,
the noisy bug began to rest,
Her companions were exhausted,
all had done their best.

All had been united – help given from the heart,
To help a fellow bug have a new Fresh Start.

The Royal Encounter

The day had come and so it is,
The Prince arrived to meet me – Liz.
My knees were shaking, eyes all agoggle,
And my curtsy now started to wobble.

Keep your calm and smile so sweet,
I'm in a curtsy at his feet.
The Prince was nice and so disarming,
He really was a Prince so charming!

I shook his hand and flashed me teeth,
Under from my hat, well beneath.
In a moment he was gone,
And moved to chat among the throng.

We ate a cupcake, had some tea,
I turned and HRH was next to me!
We had a chat and met my friends,
And sadly, there my story ends.

Geoff and the Tale of the Fish

Geoff, he was a pastry chef,
the best in this fair land,
With flick of wrist and shake of whisk,
he had a magic hand.
His curry puffs and pastries
would make a strong man quake,
He even won a prize once
for his golden cherry cake!

The years flew by
and love walked in the door,
Geoff became besotted
with Jackie that's for sure –
He gave up on his pastries
and tried another dish,
Chopping up potatoes
and frying loads of fish!

They opened up a 'chippy'
down in sunny Trigg,
Wasn't really tiny,
but you couldn't call it big!

It's hot and tricky cooking
but it didn't seem to matter,
Geoff was really happy
mixing up the batter.

Till one day disaster
nearly struck the happy couple,
Jackie made a comment
that wasn't very supple.
A man came in to Jackie
and asked for chips and trout,
Down in Trigg on Sundays
there's not much trout about!

Geoff stirred and fried like crazy,
he couldn't stop and natter,
Poor Jackie tripped
and dropped a squid ring in his batter!
The air was thick and hazy
with smoke and curses blue,
Chips and squid were flying –
even up the flue!

Soon they both were laughing
and made a special wish,
To always keep on smiling
while cooking up the fish!

I am a Piece of GI Tubing

I'm a piece of GI tubing, I travel far and wide,
I go inside your nostrils to look at your inside.
My work is very special and not for faint of heart,
I'll make this journey easy, so let us make a start.

Up the nose and down the throat,
On the trail of wind and bloat.
Round the corners stop at the tum,
No problem here, it must be 'bum'.

Now I'm going up inside,
Look out polyps, you can't hide.
My camera searches every nook,
Grab that polyp with my hook.

On we go, it's pretty dark in here.
I have a light so nowt to fear.
Erosion spotted and noted down,
I'm out of here – don't wet the gown!

My job is done, time for a rest,
Preps not comfy but for the best.
A thankless task a GI tube,
But pretty easy with lots of lube!

A Blob

I had this blob for many years
It brought no joy but many fears,
The other week, a Monday morning,
My little blob gave me a warning!

No longer brown or sickly pink
Its shape had changed – so did I think
That maybe I should have it checked?
Then came the news that had me decked!

The doctor said, in a voice so steady
"I'll cut it off, are you ready?"
I answered her so straight and true,
"Go ahead, if you must do."

On the bed in trembling heap,
With blob injected, gone to sleep
Sweaty hands, skin like ice,
Vicki calming – (she's so nice).

The doctor broke the first sharp blade,
I in frozen terror laid
Upon that bed with bra on show,
(I couldn't give a damn you know).

Very soon the blob was out,
I asked to see it swim about
In its jar of sterile juice,
By now my head was down the sluice!

Then I had a cup of tea,
Big and brave – neck blob free!
Thank you all for treating me.

Mammogram –
'Two-Up' for Beginners

Now we've reached our golden years,
Time to chase away those fears.
Don't be shy, but just be brave,
It's your life I want to save.

Take yourself, and a friend or two,
Down to the doc's to check you through.
They've seen it all at medic school,
So go, be bold, you won't feel a fool.

A simple check is all you need,
Done with care – professional speed.
Any bumps or lumps are found,
Off to X-ray with a bound!

At the X-ray out of town,
You put on a sexy gown.
The tabs have always been broken off,
Please try not to sneeze or cough!

A lovely lady asks you in,
Now the fun part will begin.
You lay a boob on this flat tray,
Now keep steady, don't go and sway!

A little squash – the lid comes down,
Your boob now looks like half a crown!
Hold your breath and count to four,
Then do the other one as before.

It pays to keep a sense of humour,
This simple test may find a tumour.
Not all are bad, and you will find,
This mammogram gives piece of mind.

So come on girls…round, thin, tall, shorty,
The magic age for us is ending forty.
Let your doctor feel and test,
So you can have your mind at rest.

When I was Nine

When I was nine I had some worry,
I cut my lip when in a hurry.
My mum had said: "Now straight to school!"
But as you'll hear, I broke this rule.

We loved to play at hide and seek,
Grabbing at the slow and weak.
This day a different game was played,
And on the pavement I was splayed!

Blind Man's Bluff the game that day,
With eyes all covered I went to play.
In my haste and all in fun
I thought – 'jump now, here is one'.

I heard a laugh and took a dive,
Bang! Stars before me ... was I alive?
My arms were empty, no one at all,
In fact, I'd only caught the wall!

My lovely coat of turquoise blue,
Had now turned a different hue.
Blood was pouring on my clothes,
From battered lip, but not my nose!

Off to hospital then I trundled,
In a cubicle I was bundled.
Two injections very quick,
First a wiggle, now felt sick!

On the table then I lay,
"Hold her down," I heard him say.
I jerked my head, nurse missed my lip,
She had now injected hip!

Soon the doc began to sew,
Needle flashing to and fro.
Nicely mended, what rotten luck -
Now I looked like Donald Duck!

In the mirror just a peek,
I let out a strangled shriek.
My mouth had gone and in its place,
A beak-like blob was my poor face!

The moral of this little rhyme,
Pay heed to mum ALL of the time.
I'd put the theory to the test,
Found out too late ... mum does know best!

The Pap Test

I'll go next week, my friends all say,
I'm here to tell you – don't delay.
What wondrous treats in store for thou?
A life-saving test by Dr Papanicolaou.

Its common name is Pap test, dears,
Let's now get rid of all your fears.
I don't know what you've been told,
You only need to be a little bold.

A simple gadget, smooth and shining,
Takes a smear from cervix lining.
It doesn't hurt – I promise you,
A sense of humour helps that's true!

There you are upon the sheet,
The doc and gear between your feet.
At this point it helps to hum a rhyme,
This really helps to pass the time.

There is no pain, now would I lie,
You just lay and watch the sky.
A simple touch – just like a feather,
I usually discuss the weather.

The gadget's out, the test complete,
All is gone from by your feet.
Clothes back on, that just took five,
Worth every sec to keep alive.

Wind in the Pillows

Sometimes in a female doggy's life,
Comes some discomfort, lots of strife.
It doesn't happen every day,
But to protect your dog she needs a spay.

What a challenge getting to the vet,
Weeping owner, unphased pet.
Getting Ziggy on the scales,
Took many tries and loads of fails!

Then at last the deed was done,
Weight is checked – thanks everyone.
The nurse is smiling behind her mask,
Mighty effort for that task.

So off she went without a care,
Touch of shaving here and there.
I went back to empty house,
All so quiet – like a mouse.

At half past four the time was set,
To get Ziggy from the vet.
Legs all wobbly, nose very wet,
That's just me … not my pet!

Ziggy's full of wagging tail,
Wearing cone like plastic pail.
Nails all clipped, now nice and short,
Thank you all, you've been well taught.

We looked at Ziggy's scar and ears,
A tattoo is now in place for years.
The ride home in car was pretty tough,
Dog in lap, wet tongue so rough.
All around my face and neck,
She's a sweetie…so what the heck!

I set up a bed on lounge room floor,
Three blankets each, well maybe four.
She slept so sound like a newborn bub,
After eating my teatime grub!

On the floor we'll camp for a week,
Ziggy lies on me when I speak.
The hours go slowly that first night,
Wind in the pillows gave me a fright!

First three days passed in a fog,
So much wind from little dog.
The lounge room smells of dog and chews,
Almost same as stinky shoes!

At least with lock-down nobody comes,
With all this wind from leaky tums.
Ziggy has recovered good,
Loves her mum as she should.

Mince and mash is for her tea,
Bread and cheese will do for me.
Settling down now for our sleep,
Blankets now are in a heap.

Ziggy weighs eighteen kilos now,
It's just like sleeping with a cow.
Legs akimbo, taking all the space,
Rump and tail are in my face!

I hope that dinner's safe in her tum,
I dread the wind I know will come.
I have the sheet around my head,
Ziggy now has all the bed!

Just as I began to doze,
I smell something up my nose!
Oh, Ziggy dropped a mighty clanger,
Rotten eggs – a doppelganger!

Tonight we'll try a different tack,
I'll have Ziggy on her back.
Me I'll wear a Hazmat suit,
Filtered face mask and boots.

I'm glad to say we are off the floor,
Back in bedroom as before.
I thought the wind from Zig had stopped,
But then I had my joy all lopped.

I lay upon my favourite place,
Oh my gosh, Zig's on my face!
I heard a noise, a whistling sound,
From out the bot of my dear hound!

Oh well my friends that ends my tale,
Of pillow wind which turns you pale.
My dog is better that's for sure,
Wind in bed? There is no cure!

A Finger in a Bandage

I'm a digit in a bandage made of cloth so white,
I hurt myself just yesterday, I had a dreadful fright.
The rest of me was sitting – watching out for dog,
She took off at warp speed, my hand took mighty slog.

The lead was wrapped around my hand,
And tightened like a metal band.
Knuckle bent, it hit arm of chair,
My God the garden turned blue right there!

My voice let out a ghastly shriek,
The knees went wobbly, very weak.
I went black and blue for sure,
Couldn't open alfresco door!

I called for daughter "Come here quick,
Grab the dog, I'm being sick"
My face was now white and pale,
Dog was hiding looking frail.

Cold pack not helpful, needed TLC,
Panadol, and cup of tea!
Lots of tears and a grumble,
Lucky rest of me didn't tumble.

Today I feel a little better,
Had some sleep, bread and feta.
Amazing how a little food
Makes rest of body feel renewed.

My bruise is out for all to see,
Hirudoid cream all over me.
Pain has eased, be better soon,
More Paracetamol comes at noon.

So keep eye on dog avoid the pain,
Maybe she needs a ball and chain?
No, just a bit of common sense,
Keep your fingers not so tense!

Detecting a Problem

I've not been well for ages,
a problem in my pipe,
Nothing very helpful on Google,
Zoom or Skype.

I can't control my waters,
the problem's getting worse,
No help coming from my daughter,
and she's a registered nurse!

The time has come to make the call,
And get the help of professional Paul.
He arrived with van of treasures,
Electric pump and other measures.

I began to feel a little faint,
But this man turned out to be a saint.
Wires and sonar probes everywhere,
Electronic squeaks now filled the air!

I didn't have a lot of pain,
Quite exciting – let's go again!
The time flew by and within the hour,
Paul stood dripping, like he'd had a shower.

The problem was beneath my rim,
This had been diagnosed by him.
The path was cut through with mighty saw,
He found broken pipe and so much more.

Sand and water all abound,
I'm in a swamp – it's all around.
One hour on and all is mended,
My leaking problems now have ended.

Pinpoint Detection are the go,
When there's a problem with your flow.
I'm not playing April Fool,
Just some thoughts from the swimming pool!

The Sad Story
of the Knicker Elastic

I'm really amazed, it's quite fantastic,
What a dog's teeth can do to elastic.
Keep your undies safe in drawers,
Far away from Ziggy's paws!

I got up early, had quick shower,
Hardly been a quarter hour.
Then I looked upon the floor,
My pants had gone, they were no more!

Now I spotted bits of cloth,
Could hardly now contain my wrath.
From floor to window and under beds,
My favourite 'Tradies' torn to shreds!

Ziggy looked from North to South,
With yards of elastic in her mouth.
She gave a flick, my pants did soar,
Now they're hanging on knob of door!

At first I was a little mad,
Slowly then it turned to sad.
Not to worry, get sewing kit,
Fix the undies…but will they still fit?

I found more elastic and mending yarn,
The patch I sewed could mend a barn!
So lesson learnt I can't deny,
Keep your pants safe nearby.

A Staffy Loves a Garden

A Staffy came into my household,
To be a companion to me.
She's cute, smart and clever,
Made my garden a swamp now forever,
And did it all before eating her tea!

I had a gorgeous concrete old birdbath,
It stood in the daffodil bed.
One shove by my dog, it rolled like a log,
And now lays on the pathway instead!

My garden was covered in flowers,
Where I would spend happy hours.
Tweaking out every weed, getting cuttings to seed,
So proud of that garden of ours.

But, a Staffy is a bit like a mole,
Gets joy out of digging a hole.
The dirt was all wet, and so my dear pet,
Looks like she's mining for coal!

I spent all last week on my knees,
Sorting bulbs out from dog poos and pees.
My hose has got holes from her teeth,
And retic all nibbled beneath.
I turned on the water, yelled out to my daughter,
Too late she was swept neath the trees.

The garden is now covered in concrete,
The daffodils grow in a pot.
The lawn is replaced by new paving,
In summer your feet get burning hot.

The retic and hose pipes have gone now,
My water bills are ever so cheap.
The bushes, fruit trees and flowers,
Are piled up high in a heap!

I don't waste my time in the garden,
There's nothing to grow there or pluck.
If you think a Staffy is good for outdoors,
Well I wish you the best….and good luck!

My Dentist, my Friend

Some weeks ago that's for sure,
I had dreadful pain in my jaw.
I soaked it in gin, I wouldn't give in,
My visits to dentists are poor.

The dentist I have is unique,
One look at him and my eyes leak.
My knees knock at his door,
I almost sink to the floor.
He says "Have you had a good week?"

Alex is always so cheery and kind,
I dread what ghastlies he'll find.
I open mouth wide,
A quick look inside,
To discover a nerve in a bind.

I need to have a LARGE local,
It stops the mouth being vocal.
Look at the size of that thing,
He says "Just a small sting"
With a smile so charming and jovial.

My nose and my face now look a disgrace,
With liquids running all over the place.
The drill starts to whine,
In upper canine of mine,
I'm stuck in the chair with a brace.

All done now, that wasn't so bad,
My word he is a cheery lad.
"Now don't eat till 2, or better still 4"
Too late I'm out of the door.

I've got to go back for more drilling,
Infection was under the filling.
But soon I'll be mended,
My ode now has ended.
Thank you, my dentist, my friend!

I Couldn't Find a Leprechaun

I went to Northern Ireland
to find a leprechaun,
I had a guide to help me,
goes by the name of Sean.
We went to Giant's Causeway,
the wind was howling very strong,
The smell of fish and seaweed
gave off an awful pong!

The rain came down in buckets,
and soaked me to the skin,
I fell off the pathway
and grazed all of my shin!
Sean was bright and jolly, said
"Let's have a Guinness stout,
There's a pub nearby –
better in than out."

I looked a dripping mess
and awful looking sight,
We drank Guinness steadily,
left pub at midnight!
I woke up mid-morning
back in my hotel room,

Then I spotted something
on the dresser in the gloom.
A single shamrock in a glass –
what a wondrous sight,
And then I felt real guilty
at how I spent my night?

Sean came to fetch me
around half past two,
So bright and cheery
"We are off to Belfast Zoo"
My head was pounding badly
from the night before,
It took a mighty effort
to stumble out the door.

The guided tour of Belfast
was busy and near manic,
This is where they built
the ill-fated ship Titanic.
My final day in Ireland
we went to Carrickfergus Castle,
Me bundled in scarf and coat,
tied up like a parcel.

The rain had eased to gale force,
My clothes were soaking wet
My hair stuck out like feathers,
I had to wear a net!

We climbed up to the battlements
to get a better view,
I laid my camera on the wall,
it stuck on there like glue.

I managed to take some shots
of Belfast in the gale,
And the dock where Titanic
left on her final sail.

I'm now back home in England,
with a mug of steaming tea,
Going over memories of Ireland,
Sean and me.
St Patrick did a great job
of clearing Ireland's snakes and pain,
I wish that he could have done the same
for all that wind and rain.

I didn't find a leprechaun,
or kiss the Blarney Stone,
But I had a big adventure
and got photos on my phone.

I've Done in Both my Shoulders

I've been a little crazy
and acted like I was thirty-four,
Quite ridiculous really …
I'm nearly seventy-four!
My garden needed clearing
to make it water-wise,
The quotes I had from tradies
brought tears into my eyes.

I didn't have spare thousands,
and so I lost my grip,
I could use a common garden fork
and hire myself a skip.
My daughter is a gemstone,
much like a super chum,
And so the dig was started –
Kirsty and her mum.

Wearing vizzy vests,
and safety boots on legs and feet,
Great in the middle of Winter,
but dreadful in Summer's heat.
We started digging in the garden,
hard work hot and slow,
Then I had a brain wave
"Let's go hire a rotary hoe!"

Off to Kennards quickly,
the rotary hoe to fetch,
When I saw the size of it,
my tummy did a retch.
We had a demonstration
and it was put onto the trailer,
Engine was so noisy,
we needed a loud hailer!

We got it back to Karrinyup,
the motor had such power,
To get it off the trailer,
took best part of an hour!
Kirsty set off across the garden,
I came just in the rear,
The sand and grass went everywhere –
a right old mess my dear.

We battled on for hours
covered head to foot in sand,
I couldn't squeeze the throttle,
you needed giant hand.
Six hours we valiantly struggled
in dirt and rising heat,
But just on 3 o'clock
we had to admit defeat.

The next five weeks were exhausting
digging up the grass,
We found broken pipes of plastic,
piles of broken glass.
The skip was filled and emptied,
we thought it would be enough,
But Cooch has mighty long roots,
digging it was rough.

Lots of tradies waved to us,
and several passersby,
All admired our handiwork,
it put us on a high.
We even had job offers
and could have made a mint,
But our fingers were all covered
in bandages and lint.

My shoulders just ached a little
so I covered them in gel,
Kept digging in the garden,
and scrubbing Pound as well.
It was late in May I noticed
the pain was getting worse,
Throwing mulch in barrow
was making me now curse.

I put it down to 'old age'
and had a Panadol,
Lots of gel and heat packs,
and walking like a troll.
And then one night it happened,
I woke up from my sleep,
My dog was laid across me,
the blankets in a heap.

I couldn't move my left arm
to turn on bedside light,
And then I heard me screaming,
I couldn't move the right!
I've never felt pain like it,
so searing and so sore,
It took me fifteen minutes
to get to bathroom door!

The garden is now finished,
the mulch is nice and thick,
Kangaroo Paws and Lotus plants
looking very slick.
The birds love the native garden –
they visit every day,
And I'm being jabbed with Cortisone
to take the pain away.

I'm Turning 70

When I was sixty-nine my life was full of plenty,
Things have really changed now that I am seventy.
My body muscles firm and tight,
Now they're loose and worse at night.

When you're forty experts say,
Squeeze pelvic floor ten times a day.
I thought what a load of utter rot,
A full night's sleep I've never got.

You are in bed with Milo and a currant bun,
Then begins the nighttime fun.
Bladders have an inbuilt mind,
Bedside light switch you can't find!

Pelvic floor has lost its tension,
Just here I don't think I can mention.
The moment of dread when you discover,
A patch of wet on doona cover!

No more Milo or tea in bed,
Just dry biscuit for me instead.
Oh I yearn to again be sixty-nine,
All those muscles strong and fine.
So sadly this just ends my ode,
I'm off to sit on my new commode!

The 3 Wise Poops

Jo went into her garden a little after dawn,
Then she saw a steaming pile in middle of her lawn.
Was it a piece of rubbish, tin can or a log?
No … there was three poops left there by a dog!

Jo's rage rose to the surface, this really got her goat,
She went inside for paper and scribbled out a note.
"Whoever left this mess on here, kindly pick it up"
Might be an aged dog, or even rescued pup.

Poo bags should be in your pocket when taking doggy out,
Don't leave poops to be scattered all about.
"My CCTV now watching precious garden bed,
Let your doggie foul yours, not mine instead."

Movement at the Joint

It's Friday morning early I'm down again at PRC,
Kirsty, Sophie, Kevin, Jane and trembling me.
Early start, more to the point,
Getting jab in Glenohumeral joint.

CT machine is used today,
To guide the needle on its way.
Jane came in to mark the spot,
A giant cross and little dot.

All is ready, local on its way,
Followed by some MSK.
Didn't feel a single thing,
Bit of pressure but no sting!

Kev and I spoke of butterflies,
I saw a twinkle in his eyes.
Did he believe me, or maybe doubted
Butterflies have lips that pouted!

Twenty minutes went in a flash,
Reception organised my refund cash.
Thanks again for special care,
I'm back next month, so see you there.

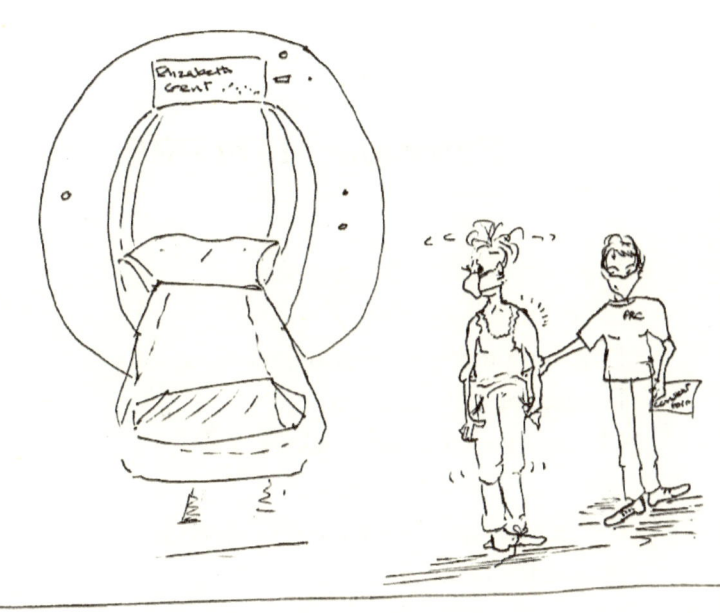

Peter and Me at PRC

I was up at dawn this morning
to get myself already,
I'm going to have my shoulder jabbed –
I'm feeling quite unsteady.
I bought new Kmart knickers
with lace around the edge,
Unbrushed hair looked like I'd been
dragged beneath a hedge!

I wore some baggy track pants,
loose elastic at the waist,
Inside out and backwards
in my helpless haste.
I wore my pink old camisole –
it shows off both me charms,
Peter said to Sophie "I only need her arms!"

Doc was really gentle, I could only see his eyes,
Smiling beneath his mask my confidence did rise.
The jab was done in seconds,
then I was on my way,
Thank you everybody for caring help today.

Me and the 'Butterfly Queen' at PRC

Doc Peter with his twinkling eyes,
And Dr Kevin's talk on butterflies,
Helped to make injections easy,
Even for us old and queasy.

Then she came upon the scene,
A lovely lady Dr Parveen,
Guys you did painless jabs those days,
But Dr Parveen gets extra praise.
Kev's jab was like a butterfly's lips,
Dr Parveen managed butterfly wing tips!

In and out the CT machine,
Under eye of 'Butterfly Queen'
Well done Dr Parveen you are a pleasure,
Skills like that PRC must really treasure.
Taking pain away, allaying fears,
Thank you, docs, you all are dears.

I wanted to be a doctor many years ago,
Couldn't do Latin – such a grievous blow.
Instead I became a teacher – of kids and CPR,
Injected once an orange, that didn't get me far.
Took some blood at Clinic, my surgical hurrah!
My family said stick to what you know,
You're too old to study medicine, brain too slow!

So back now to the MSK,
my arms are better by the day,
Lots of rest, time will come around,
I'll be back caring for dogs at Council Pound.
Butterflies are everywhere,
Symbols of life in the world we share.

My New Glasses – the Eyes Have It

I kept putting off my vision check,
Specsavers wrote a lot,
"You must come in and see us,
your vision's not too hot!"
So off I went on Tuesday,
appointment was at two,
I got there pretty early,
so had hearing checked out too.

I had to put on earmuffs
and operate a screen,
Press 'I hear it'
on a sign of green.
I passed with flying colours,
I was so very glad,
I had been shouting loudly –
thought my hearing bad.

Next I went and saw dear Terry,
now there's a patient man,
If a problem is with the eyes,
he will fix them if he can.
I'm getting some new glasses,
for distance near and far,
These are really good,
I can use them in the car.

Declan helped me choose new frames
from a big display,
The designer specs I'm getting
 will blow my friends away.
Not the boring plain old frames
with colour never seen,
Mine are very special –
 they're red and blue with green!

I'm now a fashion statement
with glasses from Specsavers,
No more being oldie,
meet Perth's very new club raver!

Does it Rain in Heaven?

Does it rain Heaven?
The thought came to me today,
Are there showers then rainbows
when squalls have gone away?
My thoughts are always with you
in sunny days or grey,
Do angels keep you warm and dry
during night and day?

I look out from my window,
the clouds are large today,
Full of rain and rainbows,
wild weather on the way.
My memory turns to years ago
when we were young not grey,
The rain we shared together,
storms through night and day.

My love I see you everywhere,
you're always by my side,
The wind, the rain, the lightning,
my tears I cannot hide.
I'm aged nineteen and smiling,
I'd just become your bride,
The rain had cleared, sky was blue,
you so full of pride.

Does it rain in Heaven
as it does on Earth?
Rains bring life and hope,
seeds get rebirth.
You are my clouds, rain and weather –
a gift from God above,
Surrounding me throughout the day
with your special love.

    All my love always,

    Liz xxxx

About the Author

Liz Gent was born in Oxford, UK in December 1948. She was educated at a brand-new Grammar School only a few kilometres from her home. Liz's burning ambition as a child was to be a vet or a doctor.

She married in 1968 and had two children, a daughter and a son.

In 1980 the family moved to Perth, Western Australia.

Her husband Patrick became a Senior Systems Analyst and she graduated in teaching at WACAE (later to become Edith Cowan University). Liz has also completed a Bachelor of Health Science (Health Promotion) at ECU.

She has always loved writing poems, and drawing cartoons for friends, health professionals and tradies over the last 40 years. Patrick loved her reading them, and encouraged her to put them into print. Sadly, Patrick passed away in December 2019.

Liz hopes these poems and cartoons bring a smile or chuckle to readers.

Midnight Owl was chosen as the title because Liz often gets inspiration to write late at night.

www.ingramcontent.com/pod-product-compliance
Lightning Source LLC
Chambersburg PA
CBHW020145130526
44591CB00030B/232